Rocky Landscape With Vagrants

Poems by Gary Glauber

Copyright© 2020
ISBN: 978-93-90202-20-1

First Edition: 2020
Rs. 200/-

Cyberwit.net
HIG 45 Kaushambi Kunj, Kalindipuram
Allahabad - 211011 (U.P.) India
http://www.cyberwit.net
Tel: +(91) 9415091004 +(91) (532) 2552257
E-mail: info@cyberwit.net

No part of this book may be reproduced or transmitted in any form or by any means, electronic, mechanical, photocopying, or otherwise, without the express written consent of Gary Glauber.

Cover Photo: This is a painting by Johannes Glauber (1646-1726) entitled *Rocky Landscape with Vagrants*. It is part of the collection at the Museum of King John III's Palace at Wilanów in Poland. This work is in the public domain in its country of origin and other countries and areas where the copyright term is the author's life plus 100 years or fewer. It is also in the public domain in the United States, having been identified as being free of known restrictions under copyright law, including all related and neighboring rights.

Printed at Repro India Limited.

Rocky Landscape

With Vagrants

Acknowledgments

Many thanks to the kind editors of the following journals in which these poems first appeared:

Academy of the Heart and Mind: "Cue," "Boardwalk, Estival Solstice," "Empty Seductions"

And So Yeah Magazine: "Gaining the Upper Hand," "Week That Was"

Ariel Chart: "Fuego," "Storm-Tossed," "All Polar Bears are Left-Handed"

Calliope Magazine: "Against Circe's Advice"

Connecticut River Review: "Celeste"

Crab Fat Literary Review: "Endings and Starts"

Eclectica Magazine: "Now You See It, Now You Don't"

Event Horizon Magazine: "Four Cups," "Agitprop," "Point of No Return," "Prestidigitation," "Rehab," "Downloaded Obsession"

Free Lit Magazine: "Scarecrow"

Halfway Down The Stairs: "Meditation Upon Another Birthday"

Hobo Camp Review: "Sideshow"

In Parentheses: "The Critic in the Corner," "Quotient"

Indiana Voice Journal: "What Ample Eyes Reveal"

In-Flight Literary Magazine: "Playoff Atmosphere"

Literary Yard: "Making Memories"

Mad Swirl: "Piece of Ash"

Marathon Literary Review: "Advisor"

Meat For Tea: The Valley Review: "Grand Opening"

Mojave River Press + Review: "Back to the Garden, Fifty Years On," "Rivers Always Rise"

New Verse News: "Subliminality"

Piker Press: "Retrospective," "Reinventing Original Sin," "Paying Respects," "Through My Neighbor's Window," "Final at Bat"

Scarlet Leaf Review: "Afternoon's Anachronism," "Ignoble Conceit"

Sheila-Na-Gig: "Chanticleer's Call"

Stanzaic Stylings: "Destination"

SurVision Magazine: "Going Long," "Runcible Love"

The Blue Nib: "Song of the Whale Shark," "Systematics"

The Citron Review: "Anthem"

The Courtship of Winds: "Hidden in Plain Sight"

The McKinley Review: "Glyph"

The Song Is: "Sound Advice"

Uppagus: "Breakdancing Rain"

Verse-Virtual Magazine: "Marginalia," "Accessorizing"

West Trade Review: "Lost in Loving Tender"

Whispers in the Wind: "Typhoon Season"

Yellow Chair Review: "Workshopper"

Contents

I. "It was another trick of the wind."

II. "We're a traveling entertainment."

III. "A heightened mimicry..."

IV. "We watch in wistful hope."

I. "It was another trick of the wind."

Grand Opening

The great exhibition hall was opening in a week. The owners already knew it was destined to bleed money, a natural side effect of lying to the public and charging them for the dishonesty. I was hired as a consultant, a stopgap measure with ill-defined duties, never allowed to interact directly with the power brokers. Still, I got to wear a vest. The lowly ones with whom I was ordered to interact frowned at my gift basket idea, and questioned my loyalties to our mutual employer. Today they let me know they were bringing in a whale. "Does it do any tricks?" I inquired. "It's barely alive," they told me.

They suggested painting it something more garish, perhaps a Day-Glo color. "These posters won't work," they complained. "The gray reminds people of winter, and that's never a good thing." I reminded them how last winter's blizzard ravaged the town, and shuttered half the downtown businesses. I wanted to explain the impossibility of their suggestions, but my own exasperation translated my speech into bird calls.

Normally I love my work, but today seemed a telephone call short of madness.

Strangers on the sidewalk began chanting my name, or perhaps it was another trick of the wind. "Be reasonable," they said, but it was a word that had no place in these proceedings. The oil painting of the company's founder was smiling oddly at me. Time was working against us, the storm tracking fast, and none of the simulations offered any solace.

Back to the Garden, Fifty Years On

Abalone rosette surrounds sweet guitar's soundhole,
but all he hears are notes that catch inside his head,
calling him like siren's song in its inimitable beauty,
driving him to be a better version of his potential self,
earworm notwithstanding, encircling him with hope, a
frenetic optimism, the likes of which recall an earlier age of
gallantry and generosity, when empathy was uncovered
holistically, when people genuinely cared for other people
innately, and music promised better times for
justice sought, an end to war and all the senseless brutal
killings, asking for peace and change and sexual revolution, to
love one another right now, and at times it did work that way,
music festivals drawing multitudes together in close-knit
nests of tender affection, singing and swaying as one in
orchestrated fashion, returning to the bare essentials that
people required: companionship, compassion, and a chorus that
questions authority, believing that there were leaders to forge a
renaissance of difference, before assassins' bullets hit hard,
striking at the hearts of doves who preached love, not war,
tearing at the cloth of their core concerns, rendering a rift
unlike any before, an ideological shift, a dream shattered into
voices that no longer knew harmony: disparate, jaded, defeated,
worn with worry and worth no more than old headlines,
Xanadu unfinished, a fragment beset with fears and disillusion,
youth's fresh-faced disappointment grown weary and old,
Zoetics reduced to lifeless corpses, along with their heady ideals.

Retrospective

The essence of celebration
caught in bas relief,
a tableau of taboo,
publicly parading the private
in ways that proclaim our distance.
Trying to digest the mood,
my mind drifts.
Strong desire begets frustration
over what goes unspoken,
over what should have been.

You secure window's lock,
wave papers in anger,
then leave them for me
as testimony, a sad proof.

Technical perfection in
numbered rooms, grouped by era.
Artsy photographs of crime scenes,
pointillist depictions of pastoral repose.

That feeling of silky smoothness
when you let me apply the lotion,
then you'd lie back on the divan
and strike the Goya pose.

Bells chime a gallery warning:
fifteen minutes to closing.
This was where lazy Sundays

were spent, taking it all in,
transformed to silent valentine
for what no longer exists.

I unlock the door.
Every sound echoes:
hollow, taunting,
yet another reminder
of distant ancient history,
feted forevermore.

Advisor

He was an odd choice for mentor,
afflicted with stoic sadness.
Years in that stone hut,
surrounded by worldly tomes,
provided backdrop of daunting reminders:
earlier days of great academic promise
never fully achieved.
Instead, real life intervened.
He had been married twice,
deserted by one,
losing the other to illness,
and these losses grayed
both his hair and attitude.
These days he doted on
his daughter, a quiet child
who never recognized
her own beauty
among a pride
of loud boastful friends.

He would pour sherry for two
when I arrived, and always
started our sessions by reading
a paragraph from some philosopher
whose work was new to me.
Perhaps in me he saw
parts of his younger self,
idealism and relative innocence,
a vibrant passion for literature.

Life hadn't yet provided
its unpredictable beatings,
and so he tempered
his jaded purviews,
choosing words carefully,
suffering my exuberance kindly.

His voice held authority;
each statement offered truth.
In teaching, he became young again,
expressing vivid opinions
on a host of other writers,
their foibles and flaws,
the limits their pieces exposed.
He had lost patience with fiction
and its self-important meanderings,
preferring anthropological treatises
about primitive cultures,
full of fascinating findings.
He had many post-graduate degrees,
framed and lending credence
to his gruff censures.

Our sessions would end
with him wishing me well,
sending me off into the evening rain
feeling somehow better prepared
to return to my books,
my critiques and papers,
arsenal of the serious student
keen on making the best
of university's offerings.
His was wisdom of experience.

He retired soon after,
perhaps no longer able
to find any to appreciate
his acerbic proclamations,
mistaking such fervid rants
as the bitter excuses and alibis
of an acrimonious man.

Scarecrow

You seem genuine enough
from a distance, a facsimile
that mimics what others deem real.

Yet something is not right
and it's hard to determine
what it is from afar.

Your presence scares off
ordinary pests, spooked by
your outward appearance.

Its beauty and vivacity
confound and intimidate.
Your directness, your certitude

are positively frightening to some,
how you hold fast against winds
that sway most lesser souls.

Your strength is what makes
you seem so unbelievable,
and yet there you are:

proud and accomplished,
visibly achieving,
outstanding in your field.

Going Long

That year the dead end was filled with death.
Our somber game shouts did little to change
the course of the stinging cold air's attack
as we dropped back from engaging gauntlet
of post pattern; the self-importance of deking
defender to bask in false sun of pride's victory.

Hollow echoes returned our voices
as raw grunts and feeble guffaws,
exposing bravado as youthful swagger.
Everything was a contest.
It seemed to matter so much,
trying hard to impress the older sister
who refused to look our way.

In the end nothing could protect
any of us anyway.
Death cheats to win,
but that's the playbook
and it's always a surprise.
I'll remember her eyes the most:
the fragile fire within them,
the promise of hope and family
gone in an instant, broken,
remiss, a target for longing
strongly missed.

Cue

She is touched by love within war,
yet makes an effort to avoid what
keeps her awake nights.

She is lovely and disciplined,
preparing routines ten times over,
pleased with what the mirror relates.

She memorizes all her father's concerns,
yet dutifully heads into this twisted world,
a naïve pilgrim seeking progress.

She learns powers of well-placed laugh,
understated force of irresistible smile,
advantages nature has dealt her.

She deploys them cautiously,
sorting out which litanies apply,
which are mere jealous fodder.

She is ready for red curtain's rise,
for whatever harsh judgments await,
for lines delivered like practiced prayer.

She narrows focus, takes aim and acts,
playing her part with easy aplomb,
a ticking grenade destined to explode.

She lets lights awaken in her
notions of pure professionalism,
the driving idea that show must go on.

She enters, laughing.

Endings and Starts

*"Spoiler alert: Ahab gets tangled in
harpoon line, hurled from his boat
to a watery death. Knowledge kills."*
This is the lullaby she whispers
into my waiting ear, and her voice
is electric, even when conveying
the limits of knowledge,
the deceptive ways of fate.
We lie naked in her garden,
side by side, facing the
late afternoon sky as I
silently pray that her parents
won't see us out the kitchen window,
the pretend Eve and Adam,
soaking up setting sunlight,
stealing glimpses at what clothes
otherwise conceal. The sight of
her breasts excites me and while
I try hard to be nonchalant,
there is no hiding this.
As she leans over for
"the ritual daylily brushing,"
her long hair drapes down,
casually, sensually, touching me.
*"If orange reflects on your chin,
you are telling the truth,"* she reveals.
She asks if I love her, really and truly.
Regardless of the flower's reflection,
I am held fast in her crazy sway.

Marginalia

The museum's long cast iron windows
let in streams of refracted light;
these golden arrows point the way
to glass display cases that reveal
the cursive precision of
one romantic poet from centuries past
who composed sonnets full in his head
long before ever touching quill to paper:
lines of perfect iambic pentameter,
well wrought and committed
with meticulous care to an ideal page
in a pretend world without flaws.

The next book is its direct opposite,
chaotic meanderings of the wild jocular Irishman
whose obsession with language led to
scribbles, doodles, lines crossed out and more.
This sorry mess of ink-stained genius,
a hectic collage of ideas struggling
to find order and expression,
captures the ongoing discontent
of one dedicated beyond reason
to achieving precision of meaning,
striving for years toward a particular vision,
a flawless Fibonacci sequence of sentence.

Standing on metaphorical shoulders
of these literary giants,
I take in the long view,

knowing my college-ruled notebook
is full of pastiche and borrowed phrases,
trite and hackneyed emotions
that my adolescent angst feels
as full of import, moving, and real.
Perhaps some muse's magic
might yet transform them
from cave painting
to studied Dutch master.

It was there in that cavernous hall
that I flew above the polite crowd
of paying spectators, riding the particles
of dusk's dying light unnoticed.
That cold afternoon I also committed
to a life in art, a silent self's promise
to keep at the simple and complex process
of transforming thought and feeling
into some memorable combination
of graceful heartfelt intelligence,
some phantasmagoric cavalcade
greater than the sum of its parts.

Reinventing Original Sin

Moody beauty, you seem so film noir,
so old black and white against electric rainbow,
all latticed lace and pretty silk bowtie.

You know how to work every angle's advantage,
the soft light of pastels and gossamer smile,
the coy invitation, the confident mask.

Nothing can take that mute magic away,
the secrets of how you apply your face,
including the ways you question yourself.

This is forever; some call it your style,
and an animus toward those attracted to it
that somehow leaves you always dancing alone.

At home in the noise of hard battering rain,
winds of past trauma rap at the window,
reminding you always another wants in.

In the end, it's still a search for love,
measuring the sharp distance between
fresh dreams and nightmares, rage and ritual,

striking out hard with pure vitriol,
then falling back into comfortable night,
posing again to help make it all right.

Four Cups

This copper beech is thick and old and sturdy,
a great source of shade and comfort,
yet I am unhappy with my surroundings.

There is great work to be done,
repairs calling my name,
paint and potholes abounding,

all requiring the kind of capital
that is currently beyond me.
It makes me buy lotto tickets,

enter into games of chance
to turn tables, change odds,
reverse fates of the moment.

Things break down over time,
fade and peel and break and weaken;
this is the power of entropy.

In this universe headed toward ruin,
I abhor inevitable destruction.
It is our purpose to resist the force,

slow it down some, or employ
those more keenly able to do so.
I sit and ponder rising ruins.

I am weary, disgusted, vexed.
I sip my wine and pretend
it is a personal gift from the gods,

but it merely softens the edges
of this otherwise harsh reality.
I want to keep drinking

if only to distract
from consciousness, realization,
monotony of the journey,

to fill spaces of longing and yearning,
to ignite imagination,
to encourage the dream.

After three cups, I finish
what had been left in one bottle.
I find another at the bottom of my rack,

a blend of three varietals,
a gift from some distant occasion,
a celebration long gone.

The source is a mystery.
I pour fourth cup
and it is sweet discovery,

a fruity, complex mix
of pleasant notes that linger.
I sip and slowly savor this wine

capable of great miraculous things,
action, thought and inspiration,
exotic kiss from grapevine gods,

liquid of consolation.

Glyph

Beyond too intense hours,
fading light trails
over slanted horizon.
Crooked vivid dreams
threaten to tempt
promised fame for ruin.
Shy smile conducts
wind chimes to music;
bright macaws
flap blue wings
in ciphered message.
You offer yourself
shameless as bribed Delilah,
eager for discovery.
Love as humbled awakening,
pleasure of rough strife
painting outside memory's margins.
You dance around
what false smiles protect,
fire burning past to ashes,
harsh talons that once
ripped you out of life
forgotten in the nest of now.
Foreign paradise
of bare bone brutality
calls like rough sea turning
and you answer, lured by dangers
that linger after morning,
tendering refreshed lie

that this empty bed
somehow
is home.

Agitprop

Romance replaced by remonstrance,
emotions channeled toward dark fury,
moral grandeur become obligation
with politics infecting art.

Sitting shivering at the stop,
awaiting a bus, a deliverance,
escape though brisk purple sunrise
to where they gather with more signs,
chanting in angered choral reproach,
that this is the limit,
they can take no more.

The lying scoundrels in power,
push boundaries of credulity,
living in this fantastical world
of their narrated prescription
without apology or remorse,
stentorian proclamation
forcing new reality,
baroque and so broken
it provokes provocation
a surge of adrenaline,
a gallon of bile.

It boils beneath
an ellipse of a smile
contorted, distorted
insanely reported

asylum for no one,
asylum of all.

This is her commitment
to resist and promote
necessary change,
for silence is complicit
and history has shown
moral outrage requires
a powerful collective voice
beyond disenchantment
of frustrated individual.

She pulls coat tighter
against chill winds
of intolerant attitude,
adjusts pink woolen cap
in hopes this message
will make lasting difference,
slouching toward Washington,
waiting to be borne.

II. "We're a traveling entertainment."

Sideshow

Even though I know they're
safely contained in cages,
the lions' roars are unnerving.
I read the number she wrote
on the cocktail napkin, follow
carefully to its real life component,
find a wayward corner of a
rundown double wide
parked in some dimly lit
back lot far from the strip's
bright lights and fast judgments.
If I waited til morning, she'd be gone.
"We're a traveling entertainment,"
she offered, sweet byproduct
of healing trapeze imbalances
and loud-talking hucksters.
She was my snake oil,
cure-all for particular brand
of lonesome hurting, one
that required limber flexibility
and an unwavering belief
in the power of self-delusion.
In the buzzing of those
failing fluorescents, I could
hear convincing siren's song.
Her kisses came hard and fast,
and I succumbed to the illusion,
sloping, groping, and hoping
right up to when her clown father

burst in from his own private
makeup lesson, and pointed
that T-shirt cannon at my head.
I grabbed what clothes I could
and shot myself out the door.
With neon memories setting
brain aflame like briquettes,
I got dressed in sad shadows
of an abandoned warehouse
to preserve the pity I might need
to someday forgive myself
for this ongoing sin
of eternal desperation.

Destination

You smell ocean salt
through open car windows.

You exit long before
envied places for the rich.

In dreams, you destroy
their serenity with pumping bass lines

that shake their sanity
from a tall wall of black speakers.

Your choice of humble dock
is not much to look at, but still you do,

late in the day, searching your soul
amongst precarious piles of used books.

The local tales hold no interest;
you seek something to bruise your soul:

a radical philosophy to change
all you have known in life to this point.

You sleep like a peaceful child,
awaken forgetful of problems.

August holds you in its maw,
hot, restless, eager for why.

Tourist traps and dives
break up long sunny days.

When you finally remember
how to breathe in a way

not triggered by anxious anticipation,
it is time to go home.

Afternoon's Anachronism

He is a man out of time,
misplaced, misunderstood,
mistaken for an employee
offering service with a smile.
After all, he wears a tie.
To an average outsider
he seems to inhabit the attitude
of necessary obeisance.
But be fooled not
by cheerful demeanor,
clever guise as effective camouflage.
Lurking within, acid thoughts
drip slowly in dark silence,
burning away
like conscience unleashed
(the little id that could).
Hidden yet
is the greater iceberg,
clever counter-force
that fuels arguments,
sidles sideways between
fancy diction and jumbled syntax,
following frustration
on a serpentine path to nowhere.
The surface shows insouciant smirk,
an errant era, a wrong aisle,
a misguided false identity,
a stranger left contemplating
how such blunders occur.
He may not be what he seems,
but right now, he's no help at all.

Sound Advice

Neko's voice is the only cure.
He plays music loud,
seeking solace through rhythmic vibration
the only way his body knows.
He is bruised and burned,
freezing in muffled cries
from transient episodic nightmares.
Letters arrive, addressed to
unknown brothers, phantom sons.
Windows frame picturesque tableaus
of neon yellow feeling blue.
Everyone cries when they learn
how so-called romantics
stole the moon.
He stands on his head
as answers rumble
through tall black speakers.
It's all broken glass and static.
The needle drops and he sings along
to a foreign city's soundtrack.
The laws have changed;
what is revealed in
the face of the meantime:
the true nature of the unknown.

Now You See It, Now You Don't

The world whispers astonishments.
Minutiae translates to wisdom
as we cross fallen sycamore,
now bridge to understanding.

Creek meanders through fog
seeking light in frigid headwaters,
answers in setting sun's fire.
Things an expert might know

never stop it, instead rush
flows toward appreciation
of well-known illusions
in secrets that nature pools.

Unspeakable beauty,
incredible horrors,
refracted through mirrors
appear much the same.

The wind shows itself
to careful observers
while imperfect others
remain in the dark.

Lost in Loving Tender

She worships cat videos,
the only religion she believes.
She kneels at screen's edge, entranced,
daring herself to be amused anew
at fiftieth watching.
Cuteness is the gospel that reaches her,
caught otherwise in messy whirlwind
of minimum wages and desolate prospects,
the afterbirth of an imperfect education
that brought a river of debt
ebbed with broken promises.
She follows other links
toward temporary distraction,
animal innocence inspiring
less shock than *aw, that's adorable.*
Her newfound allegiance to four-footed leaders
who prance, leap, jump, react,
serves to distract, to lull and numb
from this slow swirl round the drain,
boots up, waving white flag
of momentary bemusement.

Point of No Return

Two clocks
measure expectant minutes,
a zero sum game
gone strangely awry
in this indoor heat.

You stand on dock,
gesture, smile and wave,
bid adieu to what's certain —
dreams kept in books, under glass,
displays meant to impart knowledge.

Sirens and whistles herald
maiden voyage of mirrored and gilded.
Fate calls losing hand, full house
leviathan lumbers forward:
hopeful, fulsome, yet fallow.

Meet me at sandbar
beyond diamond expectations;
together, we'll cite number and verse
to catch drift of continents
before continental drifts.

Exploding white star,
nova through novacaine haze:
numb, cold beyond feeling,
plumbing depths of history,
with no midnight in sight.

Song of the Whale Shark

Sometimes you tell me
how you want to be
big fish in a small pond,
and I suppose I understand
where you're coming from.
You're not big,
so you quickly think
that might be an easy solution.
I try to be empathetic to your plight.
But size isn't everything, you see.
I know. The largest fish in the sea is me.
Endangered, but not necessarily endearing.

I have size and heft.
When traveling in my school,
I am roughly the size of a school bus.
I tip the scales at over 20 tons.
Not exactly dainty, I come in peace.
Docile as the day is long.
Because - why not?
My seventy years need not
be full of fighting.
No vicious vengeance
against some passionately obsessed
peglegged Captain Ahab.
Give me my plankton
and I'll move right by.

People assume because
I swim with mouth wide open
(colossally gaping)
that I have a lot to say.
Ixnay.
It's just my filtration system,
a way of feeding my hunger.
Sure, I seek out luxe life
of warmer waters,
but don't we all?

So being big fish in a big pond
does not necessarily help me
stand out in any way.
From deep dark bottom of Mariana's Trench,
to continental shelf of West Australia,
no one sees beyond my size;
no one bothers to look behind
what's in my eyes.

Yet if swimmers want to hitch a ride
on my ginormous striped hide,
I say jump on. The more the merrier.
Because large can be lonely.
And really, I'm happy to lend a fin
whenever I can.

Systematics

When the candy dish
fills with ones and zeros,
binary lovers bind
into one shadow,
together for an eternity
of whispered calculation.

Then man-made problems
beset men and we act surprised,
rising only to ride unruly wiles.
While clock becomes stopwatch,
secondhand second hands
move punctually ahead,
applauding this march
of used time.

With Swiss precision,
they read our minds,
feel our apprehensive
hesitance,
our distant history,
chasing anniversaries.

This is the room
where time stopped that night,
tired of weary journey,
swept up in nonchalance
that follows painstaking care
gone ballistic, unwound.

Seized. Transformed.
Head on pillow, dreaming.

Boundaries are busted
into disparate voids
as desperate illusion fades.
Populous chant begins
as if shiny and new,
all Euclid's elements
plainly on view.

Workshopper

And he breathes the false assumption:
infinite time a place wherein
he crafts phrases, hones words, masters
meter in this occupation of hazard.
Modernists mumble dead rhymes,
then turn and run, rather than be
affected, extended, emended.
He sees, senses, and aspires.
Adieu, kissing an illusion of truth,
capturing nuanced imperative
in curious ways, eagerly imagining
success as puzzled illumination.
Prince of process, each ensuing draft
outstretches, pulling and polishing
'til technique negates meaning,
and he begins to believe
artifice as experience,
this stale sheen as natural.

Subliminality

In those not-so-olden days,
they might kneecap you into submission
or try to shame you into changing your ways.

Today, the persuasion's more subtle,
minds are changed without realizing
things encountered in media stream.

They float by like invisible balloons,
banners that point the way with
bold exclamations you'll never remember.

Alone in the voting booth,
just you and your conscience
and inexplicable urges compelling you.

Foreign powers are acting poorly,
proving psycho-statistical truths,
gaining control from within.

Reading a mind isn't necessary
when subtle control is relinquished
and a shocked world wonders

how nuclear winter has emerged
from within, not without,
fighting wars no one ever sees.

The new truth is contrived fiction.
Believers vehement with denial
conjure revisionist history,

spew touted party sound bites,
and daily break what others revered
on battlefields of public opinion.

This wall of boulders
grows larger over time
until no one quite remembers

or cares who it was
that cast the first stone
or the life we had before.

And we the unsure
in the chaos of uncertainty
fear the worst world war,

not knowing that bombs
of ultimate destruction
have already dropped.

What Ample Eyes Reveal

Her laughter sings,
a torch connecting men
into bright constellations
that fill heavens
with rich possibility.
This rigid time's
demands and parries
chime an intensity,
a ticking that explodes logic
for whatever reason.
Her smile teases,
knowing and prickly,
a polished tray,
fragrant lavender and ice,
crystal goblets
decanting refreshment
of fresh denial,
hiding in corners
of awkward metaphor,
climbing overgrown tendrils
toward a western solution,
headstrong and upward,
tangled into endless morning,
confirmed through the chorus
and a hummed second verse.

III. "A heightened mimicry..."

The Critic in the Corner

The point is not reality, she said,
and it never has been. A heightened
mimicry is what the best manage to achieve.
I didn't know her name, but I could see
initials that followed her name,
indices of thankless years of
academic warfare. She was
a survivor, serious and literary,
a dying breed seeking acceptance,
social approval, or at the very least
an audience. I sipped at my single malt,
knowing the work she referenced
was not some condemnation of
late stage capitalism. Sure, it
was an ambitious attempt by
a young prodigy eager to impress.
She however was mistaking
undercurrent for surf. Churning atop
frothy waters was a youngster's
uneven attempt at domestic drama,
full of wrong notes that strove
for the universal. I was not
going to say so, lest she ask
how many initials followed my name.
Besides, poking holes in a classic was not
my idea of a fun Saturday night.
Another sip and I drifted
toward a softer memory,
a domestic setting of no importance

to anyone but me, a pivotal time
when actions muffled dialogue
next to a haunting *mise en scene*.

Hidden in plain sight

Our family packed into the Olds Cutlass.
and drove across the large bridge,
past miles of endless cemeteries
that lined the highway near the airports,
beyond the bright lights of Northern Boulevard,
past *Alexander's* department store,
to Rego Park, land of red brick apartments,
one of which housed my paternal grandmother.

Some nights we'd have dinner with my father's
mother's youngest sister and her husband:
she a tall, stately blonde,
he a small dark man with a moustache.
He was talkative, opinionated,
a fast talking wheeler-dealer that hawked politics.
He worked in a clothing store
on the lower east side, holding his own
against those haggling for lower prices.

They often had their friends over,
people who were strangers at best,
and they only spoke Hungarian.
I learned my father not only understood it,
but seemed able to add an occasional comment.
He translated for my mother,
yet I sensed her frustration,
because their talking in a language
where I knew maybe three words
didn't seem very nice to the rest of us.

Back then, I was confused by the genealogy,
unsure how we were all related,
and the unexpected onslaught of strange words
and guttural sounds further alienated me.
I would go into the next room
to watch television, but nothing good was on.

On a small porch I found a wicker chaise lounge
with a convenient rocking mechanism.
I stretched and let my eyes go out of focus,
distant trees and flowers fading into a blur
that I hoped might hypnotize me forever.
It didn't work. I didn't stop time
or magically transport myself to my own bedroom.
What I did manage was total invisibility;
I had wandered off and no one was coming to find me.
Here in this land of extreme carpeting and
creepy plastic-covered sofas, I had managed the feat
of hiding in plain sight, fading into my surroundings
like that chameleon my friend had shown me.
I sat there, convinced I might never be found again,
and that it might take weeks, months, maybe years
before my absence would work its way into this
strangely animated Hungarian exchange.

Celeste

On the rush hour 6 train
    I play a game of trying
to find whatever is blue:
 clothing, eyes, advertisements,
     because life is like that.

On the platform, I see a woman
whose expression conveys
how the world will end.

    But no one here has time for despair.

Here in the tunnels lacking sky
we share mass vibrations
and find ways to soothe our savagery.

    For me, it's the blue of that gentleman's shirt,
    the encroaching navy of a Magritte print in that *New Yorker,*
 the cerulean mystery of the jazz riff from the distant buskers,
    the turquoise teardrops of a stranger's earrings,
the color of our last salvation.

Prestidigitation

Words are easy,
actions hard.
We gather
each morning
to recount
past escapades,
ways to rise
from night's
inevitable injuries.
We are imperfect:
hurting, hurtling,
eager to share
scary dreams
with longtime
companion.
You don't say.
Diversion is
daily magic,
providing illusion
that time passes
as selfsame progress
roots us firmly
in this place.
Voices cry out
in unison,
sleight of hands
reaching up,
seeking help,
eager to stand

for something
before final curtain
drops, signaling
trick is done.

Boardwalk, Estival Solstice

Fragrant silence
of lily of the valley's luster
caught in lambent light
of dying sunset
signals certitude
of seasonal change.
Summer arrives,
all sullen vigor descending,
eager to vent shirtless energy
against warm winds blowing
through restless minds.

Life's a beach
and then you repine lost loves.
Pastel horizon
whispers red promises
that swirl and swarm,
gathering momentum
to distract and deflect
from the now to then
when anything was possible,
when long days
fueled fitful dreams.
Names became incantations
inducing magic thoughts
of souls intertwined,
and hope of shared delight
fueled sweet aches
of heated yearning.

Now the season itself
accomplishes this
slick sleight of mind,
a parlor trick that automatically
deceives and diverts back
to youthful swoon and swagger.

Against Circe's Advice

In three consecutive dreams,
a naked woman approaches,
warns against staring into her eyes.
I am a siren, she confesses,
and her voice is like a pleasant song.
I tie myself to the bedpost
and look away, writhing in agony
against the tempting allure,
yet wake up refreshed.
Today on the 4 train I see her again,
this time in a black party dress
and luminescent pearls.
She smiles knowingly,
that same yearbook smile
that once won my adolescent heart.
She disappears in a Union Square crowd,
a sea of black umbrellas blocking the view.
Wet night twinkles with blurred streetlamps,
and taxis multiply like salmon battling upstream.
I am suddenly barefoot,
unable to remember my name,
to fill in the puzzle's blanks,
to figure the whispered clues.
I am afraid to close my eyes,
to see her again and surrender
all I ever was for the ancient magic
of her empty fickle promise.

Rehab

We sit on long benches
inside the big tent
watching two-reelers
on the grey canvas screen.
I never know names
of movie stars;
their lives seem
like something happening
on a distant planet.
Scully says his cousin
went to school with one of them,
and that impresses some of the guys.
I am more excited about
the extra bottle of bourbon
that Eagle procured for later.
Drink makes darkness bearable,
makes time pass in a harmless way.
We are not really friends here,
united by our wounds,
our dejection, our eagerness
for healing and return
to former lives and order.
Narrow hallways and doors
lead nowhere, and a single
lamppost shines on the nearby helipad.
This is invisibility made real,
endless chances to forget or remember,
and a mirror that only reflects pain.
The bottle gets passed around,

and I hear distant voices singing
unfamiliar refrains.
A bell rings and someone shouts
in a strange language,
seeking answers and solace
in this complex of torment.
Shadows get buried
under stray bedclothes,
but the safest way out
is always a smile,
always a smile.

Ignoble Conceit

The century of confusion and arrogance
makes things harder to comprehend.
Existence as excuse, undefined,
perpetually misunderstood,
streams on unabated.
All the while you try
capturing moments,
grasping for epiphany
between lines of
prosaic rhetoric,
trivial pursuits
amidst tragic
stains of terror
crossing the map,
seeking your place
in the pantheon,
a taste at immortality
through marginal wisdom
and a love of language
that echoes and resounds
from a perch removed,
fostering an illusion of safety.
Does the sharing of the story
really matter? The passion
for the universal extends:
extenuate, ostentatious,
battling blank page.

Breakdancing Rain

Clattering on rooftop
all hurly-burly and counterpoint
a pitter-patter of splash
overflowing gutters and spouts
like liquid rebel,
undaunted by pale constraints
of time or rhythm, laughing to
fickle swells of storm und drang,
slave to mercurial downpour,
scatting the happy jazz
of strange time signature
then splishing, sploshing,
in lockstep buoyance
as though performing
for small street corner crowd.

Gaining the Upper Hand

It was an ordinary compact.
We reached agreements
that catered to those
beyond reason
and we did it fast.
No one knew, nobody cared,
like extracting a tooth
about to fall out on its own.
Gravity is a gift, we said,
laughing, knowing intimately
that somewhere it was already
beer o'clock.

This is an intricate tapestry of a town.
Many closely woven connections
form a fancy cloth to drape around
sobbing shoulders on a rainy day.
Men of a certain importance
help practical wives stock pantries
full of canned goods, insurance against
crisis even after the mills had closed.

This was before:
before the big scheme,
before the condensation
of morning's dew:
before me, before you.

That was the essence of its practicality.

In the courthouse, a jury member coughs.
On that same day, the beloved yet matronly
music teacher gave up the ghost.
Soon there would be doleful dirges sung
in minor key, you could almost hear them.

Once we had been her colleagues,
her confidantes back before
innocence was traded
for earnings potential,
statements transformed to questions,
when the legendary crash and burn
changed a shaken world.

Now nothing is the same,
civilization less civil,
submerged in harsh nostalgia
that serves little purpose
in terms beyond understanding.

The compact is temporary.
People wise up over time.
When she grabs knife
to peel supper potatoes,
she might well be arming
herself against violent world.

As mottled complexions
stare aghast in dull mirrors
searching for lost magic,
waiting for spring
that will never arrive,
it's time to pack up and go,
ahead of restless reckoning.

Fuego

Her fire burns true.
It inspires desire
in a small room
where desperation
usually resides.
He riffles through
photos of her past,
filling in background
stories to have them
make some sense.
She wants to shake
the world with her art,
brutal honesty
couched in metaphor
and practiced bluster.
She has been hurt,
abandoned, bludgeoned
emotionally, but she
makes no excuses,
seeks no apology.
Her life is hyper,
not really real.
He sees this innocence
in-between posed
black and white portraits.
Tell her to smile
at your own risk.
She is emblem
of new strength,

the kind that
weds ego and pride
to the assembled panel
that discusses sex
as casual necessity,
no different from
any other office supply,
a means to achieve
an end through which
new story begins.

Paying Respects

The touching memorial seems heartfelt,
transforming clichés into confessions
about the man with a fine reputation
for quality work at reasonable rates.
It was a respectable career accompanying
a beautiful family of four fetching daughters,
all present with handsome families of their own.
I feel strange here, an impartial observer,
a funereal presence with distant connections.
I work with one of those lovely daughters.
Under unforgiving fluorescents,
I admire her from the remove of many cubicles,
never once admitting the crush I harbor,
knowing she has a life apart from this.
Here I can't help but size up the players
surrounding and consoling her,
the athletic college-age son,
the older man I assume might be the husband.
I suppose she'll never know
the sound of my footsteps in the morning,
the ardor I fold neatly inside
like a carefully coordinated handkerchief.
When two fairly comparable job offers
came my fateful way, her stately elegance
was the silent deciding factor.
A pretty face, a smile is all she ever offered
and ten years later, I am forced to admit
it still might have been more than enough.

Ultimate Atlas

All across the globe
colors are names,

easy visuals as
descriptions of choice:

inaccurate, incandescent,
inchoate, in silence.

Shibboleths serve
to assert real demarcation.

Listen now to better judge,
to separate this long division.

This onset's departure
is imminent, eminent.

Stately winds of change
move artifice of time.

Squeezed into calendars
that invoke familiarity

seasonal changes lull us
into false security.

Time is only a guideline,
a distraction to deflect

attention away from waiting
until unexpected moment

that renders irrelevance,
crosses infinite border

to arrive.

After A Long and Distinguished Career

for R.B

Came another long meandering month,
gesticulations from misread gestures,
the phoenix's anger at being back again,
chain smoking hallucinations and sneering,
the vocable roar of celestial complaisance,
barely audible to stentorian memory,
stark shadows and hoarfrost,
awaiting unavoidable change,
following a pleasant miniscule jaunt
to his typewriter's promised dystopian future
under two alternate moons.
He coughs – the closest he comes to a smile,
then picks up the green crayon
and writes to his next admirer.

Anthem

It's always a question of vision in relation to light,
which seems to belabor the obvious, and yet we
quickly are hurled back to feelings of national pride
relative to the battered icon, a survivor's pleasure
that goes beyond the hard proof of rockets, bombs,
and the spectacle and commotion that surrounds them.
Freedom and bravery are only but the start, for
three unknown verses continue unsung, expanding,
expounding upon the story. From the shore, by a stream,
the silence is broken by a breeze which blows in
synchronistic concert with the morning's first rays
to great effect: the banner reflected in the water
overwhelms and delights. Pride, yes, but further
memories of confusion and the havoc of war,
the cleansing wash of dreaded enemy's blood,
from which there was no refuge. In triumph
a symbol waves, and may it ever be that freemen
stand in victory and peace, humbly preserved
by a higher power's grace and blessings,
that we answer in turn with trust and with praise.
Today we take these lyrics in stride, neglecting
Key's happy reverence for that spangled field
of bright stars and broad stripes, instead reflecting
only our brash impatience to play ball
and somehow get on with the game.

Storm-tossed

Anchored in rancor,
the silence of elected winds
is deafening, a reckoning
wherein we seek to remember
how best to forget.
Drifting into abased oblivion
as false waves crash daily
onto the shore of our certainty,
eroding truth and reputation
into a whirling eddy
of fantastic proportion.
We spin along in partisan circles,
getting nowhere, losing track.
Are we alone in the middle of this ocean?
Does anyone hear our impassioned pleas?
These uncharted waters each day
get deeper and more turbulent.
Farewell smooth sailing,
the real question is voiced:
can anyone save our ship?

Chanticleer's Call

Today a student asks if one awakened
from a medically induced coma
would feel relaxed and refreshed.
Exhausted after long hours of homework,
her wearied thoughts tend toward
such wry considerations.
I suggest exploring better options,
ones with less ethical baggage attached.
She sighs, daydreams about sleeping.
The class ponders why we measure time:
is it convenience of commonality
or merely means of establishing control
over universe of chaotic entropy?
We consider the dominion of trees,
the names of the world's many winds,
the healing change of flowing water,
the nature of the present formed
by entity developed of the past,
the journey that takes it further away
from enviably curious innocence,
mantle of the young and the animals
toward some memento mori,
carved heart from past lovers
now dearly departed, their story
faded history reduced to initials
in peeling bark, sad disarray
of unknowable mysteries lost.
Lick a finger and measure the moment,
the time of day as well of season,
the questions that prove so hard to resist;
the reasons that beauty still lets us exist.

Quotient

Gravity is a ratio.
You weigh in after
a life of clever deception.
Every day is winter anew,
whiteout conditions
obscuring both insight
and view. No voice,
no manners, no choice.
Empty expectations
in this dumpster fire
of heightened confusion.
Silence is compounded
by the spotlight focus
on the arrest
off alleged desire.
Tread shadows
carefully, trundle ahead
meter by meter,
converting heavenly position
into monthly prediction.
Horrors! Tenor of terror,
timbre of temblors,
rocking our world
off its orbit, breaking
speed limits, scarring
retinas with residue,
translating what we
believe in our blood
into proportionate

means of understanding.
Those special glasses
mean nothing now.
You capitulate,
ask for eraser.

IV. "We watch in wistful hope."

Playoff Atmosphere

1.
We climb the stairs expectantly.
The wind carries secret music, a celebratory birdsong.
There is so much that will never be said this day.
Shadows extend longer than they've gone before.

What does the shell say when held to your ear?
Does it speak of cultural indifference,
the injured who float away
after boosting the hero's stat sheet?

The eclipse bleeds a message onto the moon.
With a telescope, perhaps all would be better.

2.
This is where a forest once stood
before the rich man felled the trees,
seeking a breathtaking and selfish panorama.

The coyotes are common knowledge, their
death yaps a caution even to the animals at home.

3.
We empty our pockets before our brains.
We pray to golden idols and innovative apps.
We hum the melody because words do not matter.
Like the machine that produces one martyr per minute,
we watch in wistful hope and sad remembrance.

Present

She asks big questions:
why we are here,
meaning of life and more,
pondering beauty and horror
in seasons of eternal mystery.
Nature abhors the individual,
and mindlessness of habit
threatens to fix us forever
chasing endless circles.
She finds no answers:
not in books, not in fields,
nor absorbent mountains,
or the creek that anchors her there.
All she discovers is uncertainty,
yet she is grateful beyond words.
There is pizzazz and a certain peace
in pursuing such mystic contemplation.
We must not only accept life's ambiguity,
its lack of clarity and neatly packaged answers,
we ever must learn to graciously smile
at nature's profligate whims
and embrace them as a gift.

Empty Seductions

Within squalor of mindlessness
she struts proudly, walking down
cascade of elegant column-bordered steps
and front and center, sings, "Hallelujah,"
stretching the phrase to infinite syllables
with sweet songbird's voice.
Her satin blouse drinks in spotlight
to project this striking neon color
that fills our eyes with luster,
our hearts with restless mirth,
as if sharing a fantastic secret,
a lyrical snippet of eternal wisdom.

Since the Roman age
such performances have fueled desire,
provided necessary delusion
that so much more exists than
our daily ugliness, the quiet despair
of our mundane routines, the spinning
wheel that slows and shows
fate pointing to reality in decline.

The occasional neighborhood death
scares us, reminds of the tenuous nature
of this whispered existence. Now and then
a siren punctuates this stream
of clean shaven men and handsomely dressed women
en route to a universe of sundry paid labors,
where beauty hides unrecognized,

given no proper framework in which to thrive,
no comprehension that a little tenderness
might someday save us all.

How strange to be alive,
to taste these succulent ripe plums
and surf through endless channels,
seeking some glimpse of entertainment
to arrest time and lift us from
exhaustion, pain, and common complaints
toward a higher dream that
carries us away from class toil,
delivers us from our own impatience.

Making Memories

Tepid night invites possibility,
a chance at significance,
something temporal that might last
beyond happy moon's slow pace.
Imagination curves persuasion
as conscious singularity takes root,
knitting dark webs of realization,
hungry forces pulling unawares.
This is our time to act,
rewrite history in soothing ways,
discover hidden harmonies
extant in the everyday.
Don't bludgeon it with labels,
dissect passion into lesser parts,
rescind statements that became
mottos for stoic living. Don't.
Let us embrace this routine
as if it never occupied time,
celebrate the small death
of sweet passing ecstasy
by holding fleet thoughts
transfixed as learned behavior,
pinned into submission
like all beautiful things.
This is our gambol,
once muted risk
turned passionate dance,
step by reckless step
releasing hearts through grace.

Week That Was

The prisoners of privilege
fly off to their pricey week
of tropical hedonistic excess,
careful to Insta it all,
capture every moment's
proud embarrassment,
posing with tongues out
like antennae, seeking
to tune into perceived
universal (not universal at all),
to show off every outfit
that they starved themselves
to fit into, because in the end
it's all about looking good,
getting lit without illumination,
dancing through troubled world
with only first world problems,
then changing out shoes,
looking gorg all the while.
Shiny and stoked to show
nature's ample gifts in
a display of unstoppable fun,
for life is a hot sandy beach
and keep those drinks coming
while coming and going,
turning up and burning up
to Nero's fiddle soundtrack
and once again reminding
via drunken confiding:
you're only young once
you're only young once.

Almost Like Lent

The year I gave up curiosity
I saw what it did to the helpless cat.

Now the quiet suffices in stretches
where questions ruled imagination's roost.

Reflection tends to echo in strange ways:
uncertain voices never returning.

Take a walk instead through fields of eggshell,
scrutiny breaking everything in sight.

This is the new safe, the guarded retreat
when only the current moment exists.

What past was prelude prevents survival,
and caution crawls through a shadowy void.

Inching ahead, I wonder what's coming,
not holding on to what soon is destroyed.

Diamonds cannot always sparkle and shine:
turn out the lights, feel the spirit decline.

Typhoon Season

Waves of neurasthenic wonder
crash against imagined shore;
frazzled edge of decade's plunder
leaves me hollowed out and sore.
This is not the light of healing:
praying to the gods of sin
soon exposes bitter feelings
and the fickle mood I'm in.
So I wander out toward danger
heeding not the mask of morning,
being a familiar stranger,
leading to small craft warning.
Lighthouse guides me back to easy,
churning knots of distant past:
lovesick, seasick, heart-based queasy,
red sky at dawn won't always last.
Deliver me a Neptune's pardon,
still the sea with Triton's shell,
soothe with thoughts of Adam's garden,
back before the whole world fell.

Through My Neighbor's Window

Large candle burns
to commemorate
remnants of restless spirit
that battled against anguish,
riding out pain like rodeo upstart.

Flickered shadows animate
dark skeleton's ribs,
laughing at destiny.
Thrumming wind flies
in the face of fear,
into an ear.

It's the same old deal:
Icarus descending,
weighed down
by disappointment,
melting feathers.
Mumbling prayers
while trying yet to enjoy
view of venerated vista
spiraling down.

Desperation flaps hard,
15 times a second,
but gravity proves
the ultimate downer:
direction, a force,
an infinite recourse

beyond one's short journey.

Wisps of smoke climb,
then dissipate.

Amen.

All Polar Bears Are Left-Handed

She knew a lot of things
that made her quirkily appealing,
yet she also knew the impossibility
of us – *like trying to lick your own elbow*,
she said, *it just can't happen.*
Further, you look dumb even trying.
The strongest muscle in the body
is the tongue, and she exercised hers
regularly, scolding me against falling
in love, as if it were something
over which I had any control. I was
smitten, even though she did all she could
to refute my compliments, deny my praises,
and parry them deftly with comments
that showed careful indifference.
Where is the key to your heart?
With Mona Lisa's eyebrows, she said.
In other words, I have no heart.
She blinked her eyes as if to convey
her cleverness. Even I knew that
women blink nearly twice as much as men.
I consoled myself with that knowledge,
blinking back tears of resignation,
turning away from her latest torrent
of negation, wishing I was a snail,
able to sleep for three years,
then return to register any change
that might have occurred since.
When will you ever love me back,

I ask again, tired of this
incessant disappointment.
When did waking snails learn to speak?
I turn more human every time
she rejects or ignores me.
When, she says, *you wonder when*
you'll get the answer that you seek,
perhaps it will be when you cease to try,
or when a pig looks toward the sky.
With all her smarts, she could not discover
how logic eludes the heart of a lover.

Accessorizing

I won't wear his watch.
That's just too weird for me.
It's a nice enough timepiece,
Movado, in fact,
black with small diamond inset,
gold chain link bracelet.
It's not my style.
There are no numbers,
only diamond dot.
I prefer detailed precision
of knowing minutes,
not approximations.
He and I had different tastes.
Perhaps he was more casual
about time, given the circumstances.
Anyway, he'd understand
and respect my decision.
I measure time my own ways.

He never knew how much
time he had left. Climbing
the Hall Place hill one morning
he passed out and was found
by the commuting buddies
who drove him daily to
the Garment Center.
Long story short, he had
ten hours of complicated surgery,
getting a pig heart valve installed.

And thus began a second life
of coumadin, a blood thinner,
and a life where you could hear
the valve ticking out loud.
It freaked me out.
But he didn't mind –
much better than
it not ticking, he'd kid.
They said the valve would
last fifteen years and
would require replacement,
but there was no way
he would subject
himself to that kind of
ordeal ever again.
He made that clear.
He lived on long past
that arbitrary deadline,
on borrowed time perhaps.
That might explain why
exact minutes didn't
matter so much.
They were all part of the bonus.

So while I never wear
the Movado, his legacy survives
in my extensive necktie collection.
He always had an impressive selection
of ties in his closet. He was comfortable
in a tie and jacket. As a salesman,
that was his uniform – and from a
sartorial standpoint, he made
an effort at always looking good.

My mother's family worked in tie factories.
As a kid, I thought there was a
part of the Passover seder ceremony
that required everyone to head out
to Uncle Mack's LeSabre, where he
distributed neckties out of his trunk
until the matrons called *Dayenu*
and we headed back inside.

Dad always wore nice ties.
And eventually, so did I.
As a trade journalist, working
as corporate underling,
and eventually as a teacher,
I became known for my
ties, the striped silks, the
geometrics, the paisleys,
the subtle patterns and
designer fashion insignias,
all done up in four-in-hand
or half Windsor knots.
It's my daily tribute
to the man who showed me
how a good tie complements
an outfit, sets you apart,
and commands respect.
Every tie I wear ties me
back to my ancestry,
an accessory that
marks time in ways
no one but me understands.

Piece of Ash

World is burning with fiery unrest
while my winter blows icy trees
with wavering irrelevance.
Every statement's a lie
invested with political leanings:
ramification, consequence.
Sinners as saviors in mad jumble
of propaganda-led confusion:
denial, diversion, destruction.
This is painful shortened breath
of death's shiny new decade,
innocence piling on top of
vanity's bonfire like birthday candles,
and there's no escaping
encroaching conflagration,
mad heat surrounding:
unflinching, astounding,
increasing with age.
Make a wish quickly,
one to blow it all away.
Enrage. Repeat. Engage.

Meditation Upon Another Birthday

We all start out innocently enough,
wanting our fair share of everything,
a little fame, a little fortune.

Then, *whoosh*, milestones fly by,
each of them duly noted as progress,
means by which to measure a life.

We are warned to keep an even keel,
not to fall for vitriol of detractors
or ebullient praise of admirers.

Some drop off along the way,
unexpected victims of illness, accident,
others revealed as evil, misguided.

Some achieve greatness, or in its stead
contentment or elusive happiness,
while others grow awkwardly into

knowledge of existential void,
fickle mortality pulling at curtain
from side of stage, cheering for

better means to divert attention
through material gains, humor, or
lustful desires, even fanatical devotion

to sports, politics, or religion.
Over years, tastes are formed,
reformed, adapted or resistant to

inevitable cultural shifts
and the increasing speed of time.
It marches on, bringing

realization of the temporal nature
of beauty and grace, the infectious
energy of youth that can dissipate

like dewdrop on morning grass,
like tendrils of night's dreamy reverie,
gone in the shake of a head.

Prophecy turns to history,
as myth of potential challenges
incessantly to be converted

to achievement, to footnotes
that flavor accomplishment
in a well-seasoned life that races

single heart's beat at a time
towards an abrupt caesura,
signifying infinity's end.

So run fast, do much, remember to
find diversion enough to enjoy
rich secrets revealed in living.

Let empathy guide thinking,
let gratitude bind bearings,
as we plunge gawkily forward,
hoping for more and better days.

Final At Bat

The poignancy of this appointment
overwhelms, years spent
waiting, dreaming, hoping,
and finally the big call comes.
I'm on next plane north,
wondering what my number will be.

But reality is never quite
that sort of stale movie cliché.
That scenario is mere convenience
built to fit creaky plot's convention.
Here that call never arrives
and I board the old school bus
to next rickety stadium date.

Here we veterans of the circuit
joke about times we used to
entertain such hifalutin notions,
when talent and potential swindled
us into believing a kid's fantasies
of major league scouts peppering
sparsely populated stands,
excited about the promise
of a cup of coffee in the bigs.
That was one old bamboozle now.

Every year the pains last longer,
the swing slows just enough
to make each miss look worse.

There's no one up there
calling my name, and my parents
want me to consider coaching
some local middle schoolers.

Soon enough giving up
might mean giving out,
collapsing in some dusty
batter's box in some
unpronounceable nowhere
here in Mexico, not exactly
the glorious final season tour,
the standing O of youthful dreams.

There'll be no crowds cheering
when I swing hard at
some hot Dominican's best fastball,
tipping my cap to the
thousands that never were,
acknowledging that
in some other universe
they might be out there
watching.

Post Partum

World of overwhelm,
empty void that
draws in sadness
and drains out hope.
Black hole with tears
insufficient to express
unfathomable outrage,
injustice of bum luck.
No one wants to die,
yet it's all we do,
approaching terminus
second by second
in finite increments.
Control is illusion
soon relinquished
to irritable restlessness,
worry that murders sleep.
Separation engaging,
tired of raging against
dying light, we eat and gain
and savor pains that ache
and weigh a heavy soul further.
It's a long spiral down,
an isolation that doesn't
aid focus, as details get lost
in shuffle of indecision,
a fog prevents vision,
eternal derision is
the price and the cost,

everything's lost
to wounds that are gaping,
solution not shaping
as time screams
holy hell to heaven
and gives birth to doubt.

Downloaded Obsession

If the game ends in a lake of fire,
a horrible conflagration that engulfs all,
then what is the point of playing?

Despair is a fine educational tool,
a means to challenge the indifference
that brims over modern reality.

Besides, it's a free download
with halfway decent graphics
that encourages user strategy.

Murder is not a solution,
nor should it be downplayed
as comparable to mild illness.

Everything is imperfect, my friend,
even the best single shooter experience
leaves one somewhat nonplussed.

And that is exactly my point here:
if even our games lack satisfaction,
where is our great release?

It's the sounds of wings flapping,
of the wind carrying us far beyond
confines of easy consolation.

Life is a game based on true stories
and the last man standing ultimately falls,
but not before a tumultuous journey

at high speeds and higher intensity,
and if there's no obvious moral involved,
isn't that also a lesson worth learning?

Runcible Love

I am a sandwich alone in the dark,
ready for anything, like an astronaut
stuck ten million miles from home
and running perilously low on air.
You live in a world of fishnets
and thick mascara, wide awake
and eager to binge watch another
nature documentary that bonds you
with the planet. Some things
never change. You are a collection
of vague hobbies that revolve
like a raffish wheel of fortune.
Sunday you buy a vowel.
On Monday you weigh
the colors of shadows,
looking for a perfect match
that assures April showers bring
what may occur anytime after.
Always blame the weather.
You shout "Rabbit, Rabbit, Rabbit"
to start a new month, then
act surprised when on the 2nd,
three rabbits show up at the door,
wanting to share the good news
about the relative topography,
the grant that's been granted.
Know the will is willed hard
at last after lo these many.
So strum the pretty melody,

call the clouds by their Latin names.
I will sing harmony in
the kaleidoscopic third
adhering to music theory
in a way that makes objects
appear larger in mirrors,
in a way that vibrates tiles
into strangely appealing mosaics,
in a way that ultimately
convinces and manifests
universal entropy into order,
in a way you begrudgingly
have to admit
always makes you smile.

Rivers Always Rise

Where were you when history came unglued?

Sleeping fitfully,
dreams and nightmares colliding,
paying rapt attention as soldiers
dressed in strange regalia kicked in doors,
yelling guttural collage of urgent confusion,
following orders to search for answers,
paralyzed in deep rooted fear that
deeply poisons regrets to recriminations?

Dancing to strange rhythm,
the song a sweet melody of sinful indulgence,
your partner a vision of carnal desire,
matching you move for move, expressing
mischievous energy seeded in lust,
muscled limbs akimbo conveying
tangled tango of emotions laid bare
in raw exposure of sensual performance?

Eating a feast of a million dinners,
galas of exotic cuisine chef-prepared
for your gustatory pleasure
in delicious culinary heaven,
spice as necessary accent to
both succulent and savory,
lingering, balanced and beautiful,
taste buds enhanced by memories,
a lifetime of swallowed experience
cooked to personal preference's perfection?

Longing woefully in windy dark alley,
reflecting on all that could have,
should have been, restless for
potential unrealized, promises broken,
deceptions to one's self
summarized in wishes that vanished
like flame from candle before you?

The strangers in your mirror are closer than they appear.
Count to ten thousand, then slowly turn around.
This thicket of overgrown woods is no illusion.
Walk to the river with precision and intention;
carefully absorb thoughtful history landscape reveals.
Its magic ebb and flow comprises the journey
of the solitary individual: the one, the one's life.

Moving On

The sadness tonight is all pervasive.
Perhaps the impossibility of certain situations
and the impermanence of existence
adds a shade of melancholy beyond
familiar echo of distant chorus
calling us home, pleading that we be true
to our hearts' intentions, now and forevermore.
There's no voicing why, no revelatory whisper,
just a gathering crowd that offers well wishes,
as some move on to new lives, opportunities
for peace and happiness and the pursuit of
hobbies, passions, and dreams. A baby coos
and gurgles, immune to adult emotions
that punctuate these gala presentations,
these somber celebrations, these hugs and
greetings that pass this day's marking of years,
a mixture of motives behind tears and tributes
and privileged memories called out for notice.
Strangers and friends gather around for a piece
of cake, a slice of life, a feast of good times
savored, remembered, witnessed and digested,
with future hopes all wrapped up to go.